Denver Colorado Travel Guide

Game and Journal

By: John Pennington

Dates of Trip:

Total Points of Trip:

Welcome to an interactive Travel Guide!
The Travel Guide, Game and Journal series
is designed to be more than a list of places
you can visit, but a new way to experience
those places. This guide encourages inter-
action with the places you visit and provides you with incentives to explore more.

The guide provides you with a game system
to accumulate points and a journaling system to help record the memories you experience.

We do not provided detailed information
on locations. Instead we encourage you to
use this as a way to record your memories.

Enjoy exploring!

The Travel Guide, Scavenger Hunt and Journal series is broken down into the following sections in the following order.

Book Sections

<u>Food</u>—Everything from a taco truck to nice moderate fare. Created for moderate wallets only!

<u>Shopping</u>—Cloths, Antiques, Bookstores, Malls, etc.

<u>Entertainment</u>—Theaters, Museums, Amusement Parks, etc.

<u>Make Your Own Page</u>!

<u>Notes</u>

Food

Meal:	Date:

Name:

Who did I go with? (1 point each)

What did I like? (1 point each)

What was unique? (1 point each)

What pictures did I take? (1 point each)

Total Points:	Rate (1-10):

Food	

Meal:	Date:

Name:

Who did I go with? (1 point each)

What did I like? (1 point each)

What was unique? (1 point each)

What pictures did I take? (1 point each)

Total Points:	Rate (1-10):

Food

Meal:	Date:

Name:

Who did I go with? (1 point each)

What did I like? (1 point each)

What was unique? (1 point each)

What pictures did I take? (1 point each)

Total Points:	Rate (1-10):

Food

Meal:	Date:

Name:

Who did I go with? (1 point each)

What did I like? (1 point each)

What was unique? (1 point each)

What pictures did I take? (1 point each)

Total Points:	Rate (1-10):

Food

Meal: | **Date:**

Name:

Who did I go with? (1 point each)

What did I like? (1 point each)

What was unique? (1 point each)

What pictures did I take? (1 point each)

Total Points: | Rate (1-10):

Food

Meal: **Date:**

Name:

Who did I go with? (1 point each)

What did I like? (1 point each)

What was unique? (1 point each)

What pictures did I take? (1 point each)

Total Points: **Rate (1-10):**

Food

Meal:

Date:

Name:

Who did I go with? (1 point each)

What did I like? (1 point each)

What was unique? (1 point each)

What pictures did I take? (1 point each)

Total Points:

Rate (1-10):

Food

Meal: **Date:**

Name:

Who did I go with? (1 point each)

What did I like? (1 point each)

What was unique? (1 point each)

What pictures did I take? (1 point each)

Total Points: Rate (1-10):

Food

Meal:	Date:

Name:

Who did I go with? (1 point each)

What did I like? (1 point each)

What was unique? (1 point each)

What pictures did I take? (1 point each)

Total Points:	Rate (1-10):

Food

Meal:	Date:

Name:

Who did I go with? (1 point each)

What did I like? (1 point each)

What was unique? (1 point each)

What pictures did I take? (1 point each)

Total Points:	Rate (1-10):

Food

Meal:	Date:

Name:

Who did I go with? (1 point each)

What did I like? (1 point each)

What was unique? (1 point each)

What pictures did I take? (1 point each)

Total Points:	Rate (1-10):

Food

Meal:

Date:

Name:

Who did I go with? (1 point each)

What did I like? (1 point each)

What was unique? (1 point each)

What pictures did I take? (1 point each)

Total Points:

Rate (1-10):

Food

Meal:

Date:

Name:

Who did I go with? (1 point each)

What did I like? (1 point each)

What was unique? (1 point each)

What pictures did I take? (1 point each)

Total Points:

Rate (1-10):

Food

Meal:

Date:

Name:

Who did I go with? (1 point each)

What did I like? (1 point each)

What was unique? (1 point each)

What pictures did I take? (1 point each)

Total Points:

Rate (1-10):

Food

Meal:

Date:

Name:

Who did I go with? (1 point each)

What did I like? (1 point each)

What was unique? (1 point each)

What pictures did I take? (1 point each)

Total Points:

Rate (1-10):

Food

Meal:	Date:

Name:

Who did I go with? (1 point each)

What did I like? (1 point each)

What was unique? (1 point each)

What pictures did I take? (1 point each)

Total Points:	Rate (1-10):

Food

Meal:

Date:

Name:

Who did I go with? (1 point each)

What did I like? (1 point each)

What was unique? (1 point each)

What pictures did I take? (1 point each)

Total Points:

Rate (1-10):

Food

Meal:	Date:

Name:

Who did I go with? (1 point each)

What did I like? (1 point each)

What was unique? (1 point each)

What pictures did I take? (1 point each)

Total Points:	Rate (1-10):

Food

Meal: | **Date:**

Name:

Who did I go with? (1 point each)

What did I like? (1 point each)

What was unique? (1 point each)

What pictures did I take? (1 point each)

Total Points: | Rate (1-10):

Food

Meal:	Date:

Name:

Who did I go with? (1 point each)

What did I like? (1 point each)

What was unique? (1 point each)

What pictures did I take? (1 point each)

Total Points:	Rate (1-10):

Food

Meal:

Date:

Name:

Who did I go with? (1 point each)

What did I like? (1 point each)

What was unique? (1 point each)

What pictures did I take? (1 point each)

Total Points:

Rate (1-10):

Shopping

Name	Date:

Who did I go with? (1 point each)

What did I like? (1 point each)

What was unique? (1 point each)

What pictures did I take? (1 point each)

Total Points:	Rate (1-10):

Shopping

Name

Date:

Who did I go with? (1 point each)

What did I like? (1 point each)

What was unique? (1 point each)

What pictures did I take? (1 point each)

Total Points:

Rate (1-10):

Shopping

Name	Date:

Who did I go with? (1 point each)

What did I like? (1 point each)

What was unique? (1 point each)

What pictures did I take? (1 point each)

Total Points:	Rate (1-10):

Shopping

Name	Date:

Who did I go with? (1 point each)

What did I like? (1 point each)

What was unique? (1 point each)

What pictures did I take? (1 point each)

Total Points:	Rate (1-10):

Shopping

Name	Date:

Who did I go with? (1 point each)

What did I like? (1 point each)

What was unique? (1 point each)

What pictures did I take? (1 point each)

Total Points:	Rate (1-10):

Shopping

Name	Date:

Who did I go with? (1 point each)

What did I like? (1 point each)

What was unique? (1 point each)

What pictures did I take? (1 point each)

Total Points:	Rate (1-10):

Shopping

Name	Date:

Who did I go with? (1 point each)

What did I like? (1 point each)

What was unique? (1 point each)

What pictures did I take? (1 point each)

Total Points:	Rate (1-10):

Shopping

Name	Date:

Who did I go with? (1 point each)

What did I like? (1 point each)

What was unique? (1 point each)

What pictures did I take? (1 point each)

Total Points:	Rate (1-10):

Shopping

Name	Date:

Who did I go with? (1 point each)

What did I like? (1 point each)

What was unique? (1 point each)

What pictures did I take? (1 point each)

Total Points:	Rate (1-10):

Shopping

Name	Date:

Who did I go with? (1 point each)

What did I like? (1 point each)

What was unique? (1 point each)

What pictures did I take? (1 point each)

Total Points:	Rate (1-10):

Shopping

Name	Date:

Who did I go with? (1 point each)

What did I like? (1 point each)

What was unique? (1 point each)

What pictures did I take? (1 point each)

Total Points:	Rate (1-10):

Shopping

Name	Date:

Who did I go with? (1 point each)

What did I like? (1 point each)

What was unique? (1 point each)

What pictures did I take? (1 point each)

Total Points:	Rate (1-10):

Shopping

Name	Date:

Who did I go with? (1 point each)

What did I like? (1 point each)

What was unique? (1 point each)

What pictures did I take? (1 point each)

Total Points:	Rate (1-10):

Shopping

Name	Date:

Who did I go with? (1 point each)

What did I like? (1 point each)

What was unique? (1 point each)

What pictures did I take? (1 point each)

Total Points:	Rate (1-10):

Shopping

Name	Date:

Who did I go with? (1 point each)

What did I like? (1 point each)

What was unique? (1 point each)

What pictures did I take? (1 point each)

Total Points:	Rate (1-10):

Shopping

Name	Date:

Who did I go with? (1 point each)

What did I like? (1 point each)

What was unique? (1 point each)

What pictures did I take? (1 point each)

Total Points:	Rate (1-10):

Shopping

Name	Date:

Who did I go with? (1 point each)

What did I like? (1 point each)

What was unique? (1 point each)

What pictures did I take? (1 point each)

Total Points:	Rate (1-10):

Shopping

Name	Date:

Who did I go with? (1 point each)

What did I like? (1 point each)

What was unique? (1 point each)

What pictures did I take? (1 point each)

Total Points:	Rate (1-10):

Shopping

Name	Date:

Who did I go with? (1 point each)

What did I like? (1 point each)

What was unique? (1 point each)

What pictures did I take? (1 point each)

Total Points:	Rate (1-10):

Shopping

Name	Date:

Who did I go with? (1 point each)

What did I like? (1 point each)

What was unique? (1 point each)

What pictures did I take? (1 point each)

Total Points:	Rate (1-10):

Shopping

Name	Date:

Who did I go with? (1 point each)

What did I like? (1 point each)

What was unique? (1 point each)

What pictures did I take? (1 point each)

Total Points:	Rate (1-10):

Entertainment

Name	Date:

Who did I go with? (1 point each)

What did I like? (1 point each)

What was unique? (1 point each)

What pictures did I take? (1 point each)

Total Points:	Rate (1-10):

Entertainment

Name	Date:

Who did I go with? (1 point each)

What did I like? (1 point each)

What was unique? (1 point each)

What pictures did I take? (1 point each)

Total Points:	Rate (1-10):

Entertainment

Name	Date:

Who did I go with? (1 point each)

What did I like? (1 point each)

What was unique? (1 point each)

What pictures did I take? (1 point each)

Total Points:	Rate (1-10):

Entertainment

Name

Date:

Who did I go with? (1 point each)

What did I like? (1 point each)

What was unique? (1 point each)

What pictures did I take? (1 point each)

Total Points:

Rate (1-10):

Entertainment

Name	Date:

Who did I go with? (1 point each)

What did I like? (1 point each)

What was unique? (1 point each)

What pictures did I take? (1 point each)

Total Points:	Rate (1-10):

Entertainment

Name	Date:

Who did I go with? (1 point each)

What did I like? (1 point each)

What was unique? (1 point each)

What pictures did I take? (1 point each)

Total Points:	Rate (1-10):

Entertainment

| Name | Date: |

Who did I go with? (1 point each)

What did I like? (1 point each)

What was unique? (1 point each)

What pictures did I take? (1 point each)

| Total Points: | Rate (1-10): |

Entertainment

Name	Date:

Who did I go with? (1 point each)

What did I like? (1 point each)

What was unique? (1 point each)

What pictures did I take? (1 point each)

Total Points:	Rate (1-10):

Entertainment

Name	Date:

Who did I go with? (1 point each)

What did I like? (1 point each)

What was unique? (1 point each)

What pictures did I take? (1 point each)

Total Points:	Rate (1-10):

Entertainment

Name	Date:

Who did I go with? (1 point each)

What did I like? (1 point each)

What was unique? (1 point each)

What pictures did I take? (1 point each)

Total Points:	Rate (1-10):

Entertainment

Name	Date:

Who did I go with? (1 point each)

What did I like? (1 point each)

What was unique? (1 point each)

What pictures did I take? (1 point each)

Total Points:	Rate (1-10):

Entertainment

Name	Date:

Who did I go with? (1 point each)

What did I like? (1 point each)

What was unique? (1 point each)

What pictures did I take? (1 point each)

Total Points:	Rate (1-10):

Entertainment

Name	Date:

Who did I go with? (1 point each)

What did I like? (1 point each)

What was unique? (1 point each)

What pictures did I take? (1 point each)

Total Points:	Rate (1-10):

Entertainment

Name	Date:

Who did I go with? (1 point each)

What did I like? (1 point each)

What was unique? (1 point each)

What pictures did I take? (1 point each)

Total Points:	Rate (1-10):

Entertainment

Name	Date:

Who did I go with? (1 point each)

What did I like? (1 point each)

What was unique? (1 point each)

What pictures did I take? (1 point each)

Total Points:	Rate (1-10):

Entertainment

Name	Date:

Who did I go with? (1 point each)

What did I like? (1 point each)

What was unique? (1 point each)

What pictures did I take? (1 point each)

Total Points:	Rate (1-10):

Entertainment

Name	Date:

Who did I go with? (1 point each)

What did I like? (1 point each)

What was unique? (1 point each)

What pictures did I take? (1 point each)

Total Points:	Rate (1-10):

Entertainment

Name	Date:

Who did I go with? (1 point each)

What did I like? (1 point each)

What was unique? (1 point each)

What pictures did I take? (1 point each)

Total Points:	Rate (1-10):

Entertainment

Name	Date:

Who did I go with? (1 point each)

What did I like? (1 point each)

What was unique? (1 point each)

What pictures did I take? (1 point each)

Total Points:	Rate (1-10):

Entertainment

Name	Date:

Who did I go with? (1 point each)

What did I like? (1 point each)

What was unique? (1 point each)

What pictures did I take? (1 point each)

Total Points:	Rate (1-10):

Entertainment

Name	Date:

Who did I go with? (1 point each)

What did I like? (1 point each)

What was unique? (1 point each)

What pictures did I take? (1 point each)

Total Points:	Rate (1-10):

Make Your Own Page

Place	Date:

Who did I go with? (1 point each)

What did I like? (1 point each)

What was unique? (1 point each)

What pictures did I take? (1 point each)

Total Points:

Make Your Own Page

Place

Date:

Who did I go with? (1 point each)

What did I like? (1 point each)

What was unique? (1 point each)

What pictures did I take? (1 point each)

Total Points:

Make Your Own Page

Place

Date:

Who did I go with? (1 point each)

What did I like? (1 point each)

What was unique? (1 point each)

What pictures did I take? (1 point each)

Total Points:

Make Your Own Page

Place	Date:

Who did I go with? (1 point each)

What did I like? (1 point each)

What was unique? (1 point each)

What pictures did I take? (1 point each)

Total Points:

Make Your Own Page

Place	Date:

Who did I go with? (1 point each)

What did I like? (1 point each)

What was unique? (1 point each)

What pictures did I take? (1 point each)

Total Points:

Make Your Own Page

Place	Date:

Who did I go with? (1 point each)

What did I like? (1 point each)

What was unique? (1 point each)

What pictures did I take? (1 point each)

Total Points:

Make Your Own Page

Place	Date:

Who did I go with? (1 point each)

What did I like? (1 point each)

What was unique? (1 point each)

What pictures did I take? (1 point each)

Total Points:

Make Your Own Page

Place	Date:

Who did I go with? (1 point each)

What did I like? (1 point each)

What was unique? (1 point each)

What pictures did I take? (1 point each)

Total Points:

Make Your Own Page

Place	Date:

Who did I go with? (1 point each)

What did I like? (1 point each)

What was unique? (1 point each)

What pictures did I take? (1 point each)

Total Points:

Make Your Own Page

Place   Date:

Who did I go with? (1 point each)

What did I like? (1 point each)

What was unique? (1 point each)

What pictures did I take? (1 point each)

Total Points:

Make Your Own Page

Place | **Date:**

Who did I go with? (1 point each)

What did I like? (1 point each)

What was unique? (1 point each)

What pictures did I take? (1 point each)

Total Points:

Make Your Own Page

Place	Date:

Who did I go with? (1 point each)

What did I like? (1 point each)

What was unique? (1 point each)

What pictures did I take? (1 point each)

Total Points:

Make Your Own Page

Place	Date:

Who did I go with? (1 point each)

What did I like? (1 point each)

What was unique? (1 point each)

What pictures did I take? (1 point each)

Total Points:

Make Your Own Page

Place	Date:

Who did I go with? (1 point each)

What did I like? (1 point each)

What was unique? (1 point each)

What pictures did I take? (1 point each)

Total Points:

Make Your Own Page

Place	Date:

Who did I go with? (1 point each)

What did I like? (1 point each)

What was unique? (1 point each)

What pictures did I take? (1 point each)

Total Points:

Make Your Own Page

Place	Date:

Who did I go with? (1 point each)

What did I like? (1 point each)

What was unique? (1 point each)

What pictures did I take? (1 point each)

Total Points:

Make Your Own Page

Place	Date:

Who did I go with? (1 point each)

What did I like? (1 point each)

What was unique? (1 point each)

What pictures did I take? (1 point each)

Total Points:

Make Your Own Page

Place	Date:

Who did I go with? (1 point each)

What did I like? (1 point each)

What was unique? (1 point each)

What pictures did I take? (1 point each)

Total Points:

Make Your Own Page

Place	Date:

Who did I go with? (1 point each)

What did I like? (1 point each)

What was unique? (1 point each)

What pictures did I take? (1 point each)

Total Points:

Make Your Own Page

Place	Date:

Who did I go with? (1 point each)

What did I like? (1 point each)

What was unique? (1 point each)

What pictures did I take? (1 point each)

Total Points:

Make Your Own Page

Place	Date:

Who did I go with? (1 point each)

What did I like? (1 point each)

What was unique? (1 point each)

What pictures did I take? (1 point each)

Total Points:

Notes

Notes

Notes

Notes

Notes